HILLTOP ELEMENTARY SCHOOL

Here Is the Southwestern Desert

Madeleine Dunphy

ILLUSTRATED BY

Anne Coe

Web of Life
CHILDREN'S BOOKS

Here is the southwestern desert.

Here is the cactus
covered with spines
that can live without rain
for a very long time:
Here is the southwestern desert.

H*ere is the hawk*

that perches on the cactus

covered with spines

that can live without rain

for a very long time:

Here is the southwestern desert.

Here is the lizard

who is spied by the hawk

that perches on the cactus

covered with spines

that can live without rain

for a very long time:

Here is the southwestern desert.

He is the roadrunner

that chases the lizard

who is spied by the hawk

that perches on the cactus

covered with spines

that can live without rain

for a very long time:

Here is the southwestern desert.

Here is the tree,

which shelters the roadrunner

that chases the lizard

who is spied by the hawk

that perches on the cactus

covered with spines

that can live without rain

for a very long time:

Here is the southwestern desert.

Here is the sun

that blazes on the tree,

which shelters the roadrunner

that chases the lizard

who is spied by the hawk

that perches on the cactus

covered with spines

that can live without rain

for a very long time:

Here is the southwestern desert.

H*ere is the bobcat*

who basks in the sun

that blazes on the tree,

which shelters the roadrunner

that chases the lizard

who is spied by the hawk

that perches on the cactus

covered with spines

that can live without rain

for a very long time:

Here is the southwestern desert.

Here is the badger

that sniffs the bobcat

who basks in the sun

that blazes on the tree,

which shelters the roadrunner

that chases the lizard

who is spied by the hawk

that perches on the cactus

covered with spines

that can live without rain

for a very long time:

Here is the southwestern desert.

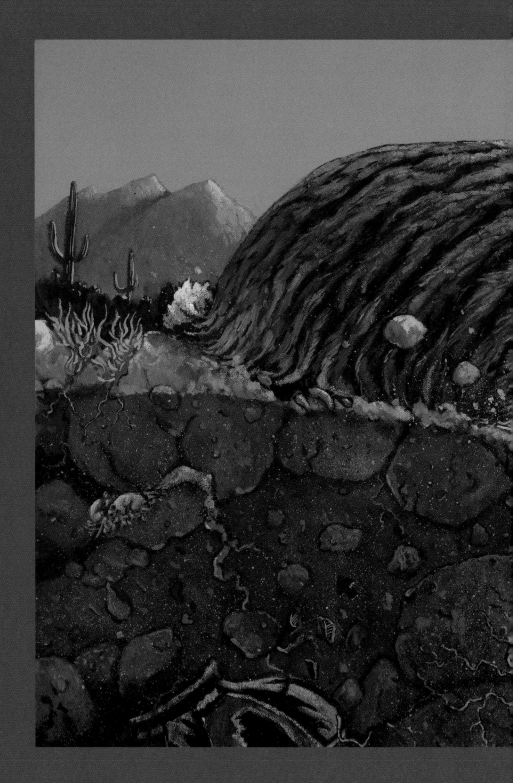

Here is the squirrel

unearthed by the badger

that sniffs the bobcat

who basks in the sun

that blazes on the tree,

which shelters the roadrunner

that chases the lizard

who is spied by the hawk

that perches on the cactus

covered with spines

that can live without rain

for a very long time:

Here is the southwestern desert.

Here is the coyote

that pounces on the squirrel

unearthed by the badger

that sniffs the bobcat

who basks in the sun

that blazes on the tree,

which shelters the roadrunner

that chases the lizard

who is spied by the hawk

that perches on the cactus

covered with spines

that can live without rain

for a very long time:

Here is the southwestern desert.

Here is the snake

that hisses at the coyote

that pounces on the squirrel

unearthed by the badger

that sniffs the bobcat

who basks in the sun

that blazes on the tree,

which shelters the roadrunner

that chases the lizard

who is spied by the hawk

that perches on the cactus

covered with spines

that can live without rain

for a very long time:

Here is the southwestern desert.

Here is the hare

who hears the snake

that hisses at the coyote

that pounces on the squirrel

unearthed by the badger

that sniffs the bobcat

who basks in the sun

that blazes on the tree,

which shelters the roadrunner

that chases the lizard

who is spied by the hawk

that perches on the cactus

covered with spines

that can live without rain

for a very long time:

Here is the southwestern desert.

H*ere is the cactus*

that is food for the hare

who hears the snake

that hisses at the coyote

that pounces on the squirrel

unearthed by the badger

that sniffs the bobcat

who basks in the sun

that blazes on the tree,

which shelters the roadrunner

that chases the lizard

who is spied by the hawk

that perches on the cactus

covered with spines

that can live without rain

for a very long time:

Here is the southwestern desert.

Wildlife of the Sonoran Desert

KIT FOX

COLLARED PECCARY
(Also known as javelina.)

RINGTAIL

DESERT TORTOISE

COYOTE

GREATER ROADRUNNER

GOPHER SNAKE

There are four different deserts in North America: the Great Basin, the Mohave, the Sonoran, and the Chihuahuan. The animals and plants shown in this book live in the Sonoran Desert, which is located in parts of Arizona, California, and Mexico. There are more animal and plant species living in the Sonoran Desert than in any other desert in North America. There are many other deserts in the world. Some famous ones are the Sahara and Kalahari deserts of Africa, the Great Sandy Desert of Australia and the Gobi Desert of Asia.

Deserts are known for their clear skies, high temperatures, and lack of rain—usually less than 10 inches a year. Animals use a variety of strategies to survive the desert's dry conditions. Some desert animals go through their whole lives without drinking a drop of water. Instead, they get water from seeds, fruits, insects, or

RED-TAILED HAWK

BOBCAT

CACTUS WREN

CHUCKWALLA

ROUND-TAILED
GROUND SQUIRREL

BADGER

BLACK-TAILED JACKRABBIT
(Although black-tailed jackrabbit is the
proper name of this species, it is not really a
rabbit but a hare. Rabbits are born furless
and blind, while hares are born with fur and
a well-developed sense of sight.)

animal prey. Coyotes often dig in the gravel near dry streambeds to find underground water sources, which can then benefit other animals. For most creatures, even the early morning dew provides relief.

Cactus plants survive the desert's dryness because their stems are able to store water. After a heavy rain, the cactus stem swells with water; during dry periods, the cactus shrinks and shrivels. There are approximately 2,000 species of cacti. The cactus at the beginning of the book is a saguaro and the one at the end is a prickly pear.

The desert faces many threats such as the expansion of cities, ranching, and mining. We must act now to help ensure their survival. To find out what you can do, write to the Superstition Area Land Trust, P.O. Box 582, Apache Junction, AZ 85217 or visit their website at www.azsalt.org.

COLLARED LIZARD

For my sister, Deirdre, who loves the desert.
—M.D.

To my mother, Mary,
who taught me to love the desert.
—A.C.

Text © 2007 by Madeleine Dunphy.
Illustrations © 1995 by Anne Coe.

First published in 1995 by Hyperion Books for Children.

For information, write to:
Web of Life Children's Books
P.O. Box 2726, Berkeley, California 94702

Published in the United States in 2007 by Web of Life Children's Books.

Printed in Singapore.

Library of Congress Control Number: 2006924061

ISBN 0-9773795-6-6 (paperback edition)
978-0-9773795-6-9

ISBN 0-9773795-7-4 (hardcover edition)
978-0-9773795-7-6

The artwork for this book was prepared using acrylic.

Read all the books in the series:
*Here Is the African Savanna, Here Is the Tropical Rain Forest, Here Is the Wetland,
Here Is the Coral Reef, Here Is the Arctic Winter,* and *Here Is Antarctica.*

For more information about our books, and the authors
and artists who create them, visit our website:
www.weboflifebooks.com

Distributed by Publishers Group West
(800)788-3123
www.pgw.com